MW01229325

"There aren't many books that make sense when you're blind drunk eating raw bacon and stale doughnuts staring at your naked body in the mirror, but this seems to be one of them. It's a starved dog's logic about bones, a dry bill found on the sidewalk after a rainstorm, a burning man's lust for a swimming pool, and the silver lining to betting your whole paycheck on a horse you watched break a leg and get shot on the home stretch. The harsh reality of it is right there in front of you uncomplicated, daring you to either flinch or smile."

 - Ezhno Martin; Editor of EMP Books, writer of many horrible poems about being a worse person, and habitual eater of raw bacon in the nude

Dark Heart Press
www.darkheartpress.com

Logo by tommy

ISBN: 979-8-88596-417-3

CENTAUR

Jonathan S Baker
Tony Brewer

Dark Heart Press

CONTENTS

Jonathan S Baker

Tony Brewer

MAN

Horse sense is the thing a horse has which keeps it from
betting on people.
—W. C. Fields

Maryland Street Lounge

asymmetrical angels
pass looks on trays
perfumed with sweat

frost blasted beverages
white over yellow
tap purified water

quarters as weapons
warbling full force
warped country records

Fast Eddy's

live audiences wait
for prerecorded echoes
to fade in porcelain stalls

a captive crowd
lined up to spill their drinks
when in she saunters

bedlam's princess
squats to kiss the drain
with salted lips

Sportsman's

green tiled entrances
make way burgers
step aside guitar

corners held with coins
green felt tables
for victory feasts

horseradish voices
call for backway exits
into gravel pastures

Sarto Catholic Retreat

grass fields between
the rectory and the classes
three of us spoke with wine
in each other's arms
she asked for the two of us
and I lost nerve
only with others
did I ever go back

The Corner Bar

hopped a train car packed
the air sopping wet
the walls breathing
migrants shared a song
and we made it home safe

The Third Base Bar

nostalgic sadsacks
belt out common memories
crying over where we weren't

Breaker's

soft violet liquid
smashes boundaries
between her and me

low throbbing rhythms
erased the distance
between her and me

harsh dancing light
hides realities
of us, her and me

West Side Liquor

walking distance from
couch crashing
roadside service
nearly home
where the Tigris and Euphrates meet

PG

a starting point
too late for me
smelling of mold
anarchists
holding no regard
masters or accountability

Lamasco's

we were beautiful and sacred
there and only there
with the po' folks
at one thousand degrees
and under my wife's gaze
and never again

County Roads

thick smoke rolls from
from a loud orange wagon's windows
as a sap chauffeurs a fiend
pressing young girls too far
through tall rows of corn

angry sheriffs watch
as a punk kid pours til
fields are mudded
to keep his beer
from wetting their lips

stumbling blind drunk
his tractor hauls us back to the ditch
and tows out her car
so I can save face
at least I change the tire

SPE

exaggerated art of desire
in full living color
glorious beautiful degenerates
sequined tucked and painted
tactless crass piece of hot drag ass
on the main stage
under the smokers awning
a taboo kiss as she watches
from behind the curtain
it felt just as right as every other first kiss

Baby Doll's

this is her second gig
dancing for moist bills
after making change all day
at the wrong end
of a one way street
at the door stands a bouncer
who reminds drunks
to pull out the right way
no cover at the door
no doors on the private area
everything washed in soft pink

Ed's Fire

backwards backwoods Ed
spraying fuel on the bonfires
instead of talking to girls
or boys or whatever
never trying to get his wic wet
just standing there staring
flames mirrored on his thick cut glasses
balanced on a face
carved from a log of bologna
giving the fire looks
the way a burning man
might lust after a swimming pool

Indy

training to be upstanding businessmen
we took breaks to be the worst people we could be
and now I think about how
for most how low they could stoop
was a sign of how successful they would become

The Bishop

chemically induced vulnerability
brought out old sadness at being ugly
I nearly wept before my heroes
I couldn't have been happier about it

HORSE

". . . lack of communication with horses has impeded human progress," said Abrenuncio. "If we ever broke down the barriers, we could produce the centaur."
—Gabriel Garcia Marquez

Table Talk

My turn: I don't have religion
walked away without incident
same time Dad quit going
around fourteen or fifteen
Who wouldn't want to lay
on the couch reading Sunday funnies
and watch Star Trek instead?

(A barely perceptible awkward silence
as the Lutheran poet and Catholic poet
and Quaker poet and Buddhist – finally
all other faiths exhausted – poet
chew food stare at half-empty
or empty wine glasses)

My ex was a solitary witch
I tried but I suck
at cooking and spellwork
Nicked myself with athames
took everything literally

(A hint of recognition when
conversation shifts to
our students for I have
none and listen without jade)

I think I settled on typewriters
and time as iconography

Picked some freaks for patron saints
They're mostly self-destructive
Some self-deconstructive
Some are Jewish

(A certain carefulness with heathens
who may not have read
all the right good books
Left behind li'l wannabe vitki
who preferred not to convert)

No just a bachelor's
Mentors did not push MFA
and I felt done with school just then
done with everything no church
no steeple no beliefs no people
Raising chickens chopping wood poetry

(A European city is named
We've all been there I lie not
sure not as an adult counts)

Keep writing till you've nothing to say
Keep submitting till acceptance
then submit more
is how everybody does it anyway right?

(A racket of faith)

The Miracle of the Dry Dollars

I found a dry dollar bill on the street after a rainstorm
and almost did not pick it up but did
A few feet later I saw another
dry as a bone next to a sidewalk puddle
I snagged it too and thought yeah!
2 dollars is not much but I was gaining
and the parking meter had already
charged my app so I pocketed
the largesse and hoped to see

an opportunity to turn this into
a parable of luck/privilege/
compassion after the downpour
the miracle of the dry dollars
beneath my sodden shoes
but it was a short walk to my car
and as luck would have it
there was no one on the street
just then to give it to
and the sun came out and the wind
picked up in a flinty sky

It was glorious and I was richer
so I put all the windows down
and big trucks splashed sprinkles
at my face and windshield
and I drove back to work

Later I rounded up
the charge on my electricity bill
to help pay someone else's
and later did the same
for a sandwich at the co-op
the overage going to the food bank
while the bearded checkout dude
said thank you without cracking smile

Loving the job

My furnace guys jerk
each other around
friends longer than marriage
and they spar "like
an old couple" says Ron
I was thinking comedy duo routine
the artificial back-and-forth
of bickering without malice
requiring no setup
You know how this one goes:
old couple fighting
telling you it's normal
means they've lost the words for love
if they ever had them
Grown into the grade school
shoulder punch
Insults raining like tiny kisses
but an occasional peck on the cheek
Mom and Dad were like
nothing I'd ever laughed at
She hysterical in his
invisible stranglehold
while he bitched out her every move
Me in the belly of it
burning gently like a pilot light
That's how I relate to people
Are you serious or joking?
Did I buy a ticket to a show
or are we related?

Jokes aside they do good work
with one-year labor guarantee

Kids Table Again

Tradition is a pile of excuses
pulled into the future
like feathers and bowling balls
falling at the same speed in a vacuum
Observable and unchangeable
and everyone knows
what will happen
In fact they are counting on it
No kids, no family, an anomaly
though the Brewers also include
a long line of bachelor uncles
I push myself back from meals now
all my problems right up here
instead of playing out
across offspring of generations
They don't make 'em
like they used to is the lie
There is no other way
or should not be and
they are terrified
I suggest it

No shame No name No blame

Safe Haven Baby Box is a device where birth mothers can safely, securely, and anonymously surrender their babies if they cannot care for them.

Mom	Baby	Box
Somewhere silent alarms	Grandma's oven	I know one thing
sound in threes	a tortuous creak	how they disappear
I forget they're automatic	when the door opened	like sugar into cake
every time you enter me	I lived that kitchen	Thoughts and prayers
many tears	warmer than the house	make problems appear
and pep talks	before I knew anything	to go away
seduce acceptance	everything a gift	I have a handle on this
I don't know anymore	my crisis situation	and lock
or want to be known	somewhere someone keeps	no second thought
the face-to-face	my footprints safe	a prison pass-through
surrender of love	stay with me stay	employees on the inside
abandons me	three minutes eternity	mom on the out
I cannot breathe	I will not remember	the controlled climate
without waking	the bolt slamming home	of last resort
into inescapable	smiles and cries reflex	built only for this
survival	it's just Grandma's oven	hatched love
I cannot	then the dark	puts forgetting into
have to		opens and closes
do this now		like a trap

Mind Game

Staring intently & thinking
of oranges to get her
to dream of oranges

In my mind she wakes
raw pulp between sucked teeth
smacking at bittersweet
the tang of her I taste
when I recall but
she is far away

Then she really wakes
& whispering oranges
to plant a dream
in her sleep did not work

I taste vaguely
of last night's supper
rise quickly & brush away
what she'd rather not kiss

Sunshine is a drug

My trees spike dirty skin
to let tiny breaths out
Quick gasps of centuries
little black lung spots

Nothing metaphors
like mammals aware
Here the dark turn
the night not normal
but cover lovers weather

Everything happens broad
equally small quiet night

The night an alignment
of souls resting atop souls
in perfected silhouette
all burning yet
the heat feels cold

Its moving always moving
stop unimaginable
all the garbage all the nukes
& love & sensitivity
fit infinitely into it

The insatiable furnace of you
destined to burn & built

to someday beyond all death
wink out like a goddamn
nod off quit

It happens sometimes every time

One day the Earth began to swallow whole
cars disappearing into parking lot holes
a literal mouth with actual teeth & screaming.

It came on sudden like silence.
A rumble where the ground cracked
open like a grin & I swear a gulp, said eyewitnesses.

Then the whole scene went back to normal.
People abandoned their empty shopping
carts & drove off as usual.
A ton of cops showed up mere minutes
after danger had passed & shook their heads
& took statements & told the media to stay back.
Everybody stand back.

I'm on my BMX bike on an overlooking hill.
12 watching people freak out.
Someone they love has disappeared
Reality dawned that now there is time to fret.

The sky was never not the sky but
you could focus on a better sky
with worst-case-scenario brain occupied.

Protecting those you love you lose sight of that
forever worrying about success.
But when your baby slides into a deep crevice

& then the Earth closes over them again & the tongue

of nature licks its lips as if that baby was delicious
the amount of grief is both monumental & minimal.
Who the hell would expect that, one might be thinking
& yet with no one – no person to blame or incarcerate

man – what a liberating prospect – losing a loved one
& gaining time to think on what really matters:
ensuring future generations are able to breathe.

At least that's what it looked like from up here
as I tapped a Marlboro out of the pack and lit it

with free matches they used to give you at the gas station.
I was not a political kid just then but
I absolutely could imagine a better world than this.

bayside bridge eclipse 2018

Driving across the bayside bridge with early commuters
I was struck by the twin on my left
partially obscured by the sun yet to rise
Blood red and enormous in its Gulf cradle
I am so small in my rental car alone in three lanes
weaving slightly as I crane my neck to glimpse
the last one of these for 150 years
Not as miniscule as the pelicans flying
parallel in the opposite direction too intent to look
too busy with belly-can ways of fish for food
but aware the moon has its effects
As I am drawn to it as their meals
collect into rising tide schools
Rising sun escaping the Tampa teeth east
Early commuters wending toward job sites
in packs of banged up white crew cab trucks
the current of the bridge traffic pulling us
in waves of human rhythm toward another dawn
as another special moon disappears

Colophon Condensed

And finally, a little tombstone of text at the end
describing the typeface and its maker and when it was cut
and then remade for WYSIWYG and plastic keys.

This book was specially designed
by human beings for human beings,
with a skill dating back all the way to 1977,
or, if you want to get technical, 1544.
The body was set in ITC Unicorn Rampant
with headers in Dirty Bomb Bold,
feet and folios in Cadaverous Italic.
Printed on left-hand rolled sheets of 69#
Roman Hammer Baked Pus Slight Opaque,
by Goody Goody & Sons, Ltd.

It says so right there in print,
so it must be true, like the Bible.
Hand, eye, and ego disappear into ink and steel
until the skin begins to glow and stain like deckled
leaves.

A seed's origin historians and botanists
surely would wither without knowledge of,
but when you sit down to dinner,
it's what's on your plate and how it tastes that matter.

Go ask a gardener how his hands got dirty.
He won't sell you a recipe for dirt.

Yet there they are: all the secrets of a book
when I could almost believe the text
had been set by lightning burning
words into the backside of a tree
felled, stripped, folded, gathered, and trimmed
by the honest hands of a modest god
who miraculously designed the pages

so when typos creep in, it's through fault of man,
the author's haste, an editor's migraine,
a nameless, faceless typesetter's sloppy sin.

ACKNOWLEDGMENTS

Fast Eddy's appears in *Pressure* from Two Key Customs
Lamasco's appears in the pages of *Clutch*
County Roads and **Ed's Fire** have appeared in
Lothlorien Poetry Journal
The Bishop has appeared in the pages of *Seppuku*

Loving the job appears in *Gasconade Review 8: Wolf at the Door/Nobody Home*
Sunshine is a drug appears in *Pity for Sale* from Gasconade Press (2022)
bayside bridge eclipse 2018 appears in *Dancing Beneath Damian Rucci's Moon*

JONATHAN S BAKER lives and works in Evansville, Indiana, where they are the host and organizer of Poetry Speaks, Indiana's longest running poetry series. They are also the co-editor at The Grind Stone and editor-in-chief at Pure Sleeze Press. They have published 12 books of poetry including Cock of the Walk (Laughing Ronin Press, 2022), Raised in the TV (The Grind Stone, 2022), Long Nights in Stoplight City (Between Shadows Press, 2023), and Pressure (Two Key Customs, 2023).

Feel free to send them compliments at
Jonathan.s.baker@gmail

TONY BREWER is a poet and audio artist from Bloomington, Indiana, where he is executive director of the Spoken Word Stage at the 4th Street Festival and co-producer of the Writers Guild Spoken Word Series and the Urban Deer Performance Series. He has published 12 books and chapbooks including *Good Job, Lightning* (Stubborn Mule Press, 2024), *Fragile Batteries* (The Grind Stone, 2023), *Pity for Sale* (Gasconade Press, 2022), *Homunculus* (Dos Madres Press, 2019), and *Hot Type Cold Read* (Chatter House Press, 2013). Tony has been offering Poetry On Demand at coffeehouses, museums, cemeteries, churches, bars, and art and music festivals for over a decade, and he is a frequent collaborator with experimental music & field recording ensemble ORTET.

linktr.ee/TonyBrewer

Made in the USA
Columbia, SC
18 June 2024